THE WALTONS

Irish Songbook

VOLUME I

Waltons

PUBLISHING

Music Setting & Arrangement • Gregory Magee
Cover Design • Temple of Design
Cover Photo • Bord Fáilte

Order No. wm1328
ISBN No. 1 85720 1132

Exclusive Distributors:
Walton Manufacturing Co. Ltd.
Unit 6A, Rosemount Park Drive, Rosemount Business Park,
Ballycoolin Road, Dublin 11, Ireland

The James Import Company
500 Saw Mill River Road, Yonkers, NY 10701, USA

Printed in Ireland by ColourBooks Ltd.

1 3 5 7 9 0 8 6 4 2

Contents

The Dublin Saunter

Words & Music by Leo Maguire

I've been north and I've been south and I've been east and west, I've been just a roll-ing stone. Yet there's one place on this earth I've al-ways liked the best, Just a lit-tle town I call my own.

Chorus Dub-lin can be hea-ven, with

come and meet me there, In Dub - lin on a sun - ny sum - mer morn - ing.

I've been here and I've been there,
I've sought the rainbow's end,
But no crock of gold I've found.
Now I know that come what will,
Whatever fate may send,
Here my roots are deep in friendly ground.
CHORUS

Grafton Street, Dublin

The Homes of Donegal

Words & Music by Séan MacBride

I've just stepped in to see you all, I'll
on — ly stay a while.
want to see how you're get - tin' on, I

want to see your smile. I'm

hap - py to be back a - gain, I

greet you big and small. For there's

no place else on earth just like the

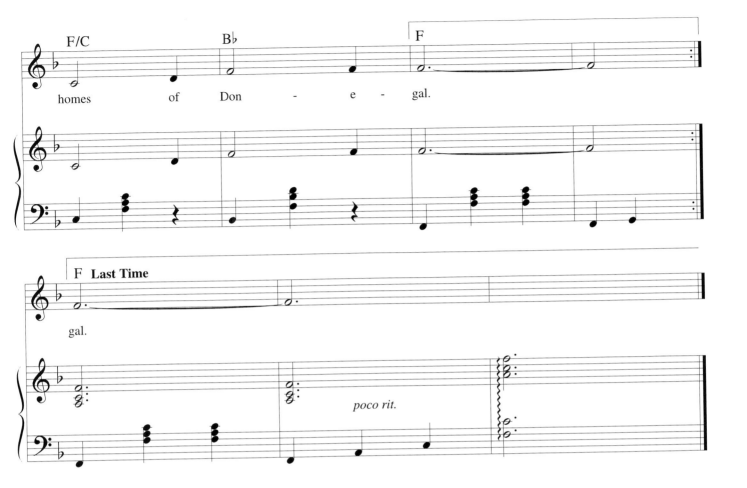

homes   of   Don - e - gal.

gal.

poco rit.

To see your homes at parting day, of that I never tire,
And hear the porridge bubblin' in a big pot on the fire,
The lamp alight, the dresser bright, the big clock on the wall.
O, a sight serene, celestial scene in the homes of Donegal.

I long to sit along with you and while away the night,
With tales of yore and fairy lore beside your fires so bright,
And then to see prepared for me a shake-down by the wall.
There's repose for weary wand'rers in the homes of Donegal.

Outside the night winds shriek and howl, inside there's peace and calm,
A picture on the wall up there's our Saviour with a lamb,
The hope of wandering sheep like me and all who rise and fall.
There's a touch of heavenly love around the homes of Donegal.

A tramp I am and a tramp I've been, a tramp I'll always be,
Me father tramped, me mother tramped, sure trampin's bred in me.
If some there are my ways disdain and won't have me at all,
Sure I'll always find a welcome in the homes of Donegal.

The time has come and I must go, I bid you all adieu,
The open highway calls me forth to do the things I do.
And when I'm trampin' far away I'll hear your voices call,
And please God I'll soon return unto the homes of Donegal.

The Boston Burglar

Traditional

Lyrics:
I was born and bred in Boston, a place you all know well, Brought up by honest parents, the truth to you I'll tell, Brought

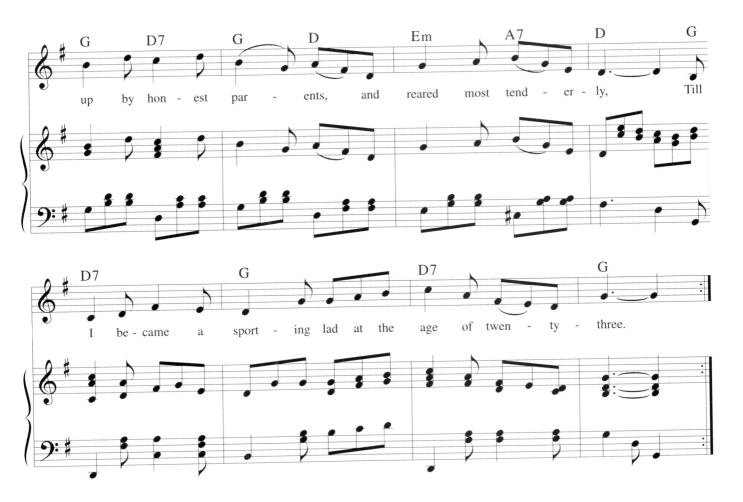

up by hon-est par - ents, and reared most tend - er - ly, Till

I be-came a sport - ing lad at the age of twen - ty - three.

My character was broken and I was sent to jail,
My friends and parents did their best to get me out on bail.
But the jury found me guilty and the judge he wrote it down,
'For the breaking of the Union Bank you are sent to Charlestown!'

I can see my dear old father standing at the bar,
Also my own dear mother was tearing out her hair,
Tearing out her old grey locks and the the tears came tumbling down.
'My son, my son, what have you done to be sent to Charlestown?'

I set my foot on an east-going train one cold December day.
In every station I passed by I could hear the people say,
'There goes the Boston Burglar, in strong irons he is bound,
For the breaking of the Union Bank he is sent to Charlestown.'

There's a girl in Boston city, a girl that I know well,
And if e'er I get my liberty with her I mean to dwell.
If e'er I get my liberty rough company I will shun,
Likewise the walking of the streets, likewise the drinking of rum.

Now you that have your liberty, pray keep it if you can,
And don't go midnight rambling or you'll break the laws of man.
And if you do you're sure to rue and you'll find yourself like me,
A-sentenced down to twenty years of penal servitee.

My Irish Molly O

Words & Music by William Jerome & Jean Schwartz

Molly dear, now did you hear, I furnished up the flat,
Three little cosy rooms with bath and 'welcome' on the mat.
It's five pounds down and two a week, we'll soon be out of debt,
It's all complete except they haven't brought the cradle yet.
CHORUS

The Irish Rover

Adapted by Joseph Crofts

On the fourth of Ju- ly eight-een hun-dred and six, we set sail from the sweet cove of

Cork. We were sail - ing a-way with a carg - o of bricks, for the grand ci - ty hall in New

York. 'Twas a won - der - ful craft, she was rigg'd fore and aft, and

We had one million bags of the best Sligo rags, we had two million barrels of stone,
We had three million sides of ould blind horses' hides, we had four million barrels of bone.
We had five million hogs, we had six million dogs, we had seven million barrels of porter,
We had eight million bales of ould nanny goats' tails on board the Irish Rover.

CHORUS (repeat after each verse):
So fare thee well, my own true love, I'm going far from you,
And I swear by the stars above, forever I'll be true to you.
Though as I part it breaks my heart, yet when the trip is over,
I'll come back again in true Irish style, aboard the Irish Rover.

There was ould Mickey Coote who played hard on his flute when the ladies lined up for a set.
He would tootle with skill for each sparkling quadrille, till the dancers were fluthered and bet.
With his smart witty talk he was 'Cock o' the Walk' as he rowled the dames under and over.
When he took up his stance they all knew at a glance that he sailed the Irish Rover.

There was Barney Magee from the banks of the Lee, there was Hogan from county Tyrone,
And Johnny McQuirk who was scared stiff of work, and a chap from Westmeath named Malone.
There was Slugger O'Toole who was drunk as a rule, and fighting Bill Tracy from Dover,
There was Dolan from Clare just as strong as a bear, all on board the Irish Rover.

For a sailor it's always a botherin' life, it's so lonesome by night and by day,
That he longs for the shore and a charming young wife, who will melt all his troubles away.
All the noise and the rout, swillin' poteen and stout, for him soon is done and over.
Of the love of a maid he is never afraid, that ould salt from the Irish Rover.

We had sailed seven years when the measles broke out, our ship lost its way in the fog,
Then the whale of a crew were reduced down to two, myself and the captain's ould dog.
The ship struck a rock, O Lord what a shock, the boat was turned right over,
Whirled nine times around, then the ould dog was drowned, I'm the last of the Irish Rover.

I'm the last of the barons, those 'buckos' so tough, an ould salt who has weathered the storm.
Be the breezes asleep, or the sea wild and rough, we were always in top fighting form!
Oh 'tis we were the boys who had tasted life's joys, on shore we were all in clover,
For all women and wine, so buxom and fine, loved the lads of the Irish Rover.

The Square and Cathedral, Queenstown (now Cobh), County Cork

Molly Bawn and Brian Oge

Words & Music by Cathal MacGarvey

Oh come lis-ten to my sto-ry, Mol-ly Bawn, I'm bound for death or glo-ry, Mol-ly Bawn, For I've list-ed in the ar-my where those eyes no more can harm me, faith they kill me while they charm me, Mol-ly Bawn. Mush-a Bri-an you've been drink-ing now you

'Twas yourself that drove me to it, Molly Bawn,
When you read my death you'll rue it, Molly Bawn.
When I die 'mid foemen wrestling and the balls like hail are whistling
And the bloody bayonets bristling, Molly Bawn.
Sure the last words I'll be speakin', Molly Bawn,
When my soul its leave is takin', Molly Bawn,
Will be gra machree my sthoreen, your sweetheart Brian Oreen,
For you his blood is pouring, Molly Bawn.

Sure I did it all to prove ye, Brian Oge,
For I hate, och no I love you, Brian Oge.
But keep up your heart a chora, sure I'll buy you out tomorrow
Or I'll die of shame and sorrow, Brian Oge.
And to think that you should doubt me, Brian Oge,
And myself just wild about ye, Brian Oge.
Would you let that thief Phil Doreen come and wed me in the mornin',
Faith ye might have giv'n me warning, Brian Oge.

Oh I'm strong and hale and hearty, Molly Bawn,
I'm one like Bonaparty, Molly Bawn.
Sure the divil a list I listed for the sargeant tried but missed it,
You are mine, now you've confessed it, Molly Bawn.
Oh I'm kilt outright with shamin', Brian Oge.
'Tis yourself that knows its shamin', Brian Oge.
BOTH:
But as (you/I) didn't take the shillin' just to save (yer/my) life (I'm/you're) willin'.
We'll get wed, (behave ye/sure I'm no) villain (Brian/Misthress) Oge.

Courting Couple, Blarney, County Cork

The Good Old Days

Words & Music by Cyril Curran

I re-mem-ber well the years gone by and the chang-es they have brought. I've lived right here in the Em'-rald Isle since I was just a tot, And grand-pa-pa in his po-ny trap on a Sun-day could be seen, But the

po - ny trap's now out of date; 'Tis the fast - going Lim - ous - ine.

Chorus

Do you re - mem - ber the good old days, for - ever they are past. They'll

nev - er be the same a - gain, for things are chang - ing fast.

The low back car, the rocking chair, the tandem made for two,
Fond memories of years gone by, today they are so few.
Our present need is rush and speed, they travel night and day.
The foreign land has lent a hand, the curse is here to stay.
CHORUS

The grass grows green, the Shamrock seen, the mountains stand so tall.
They're always there, beyond compare, they never change at all.
The friends we knew are still so true and will be to the end.
I'd give this world if years gone by could be renewed again.
CHORUS

Blackrock, County Dublin

Cockles and Mussels (Molly Malone)

Traditional

In Dub - lin's fair cit - y, where the girls are so prett - y, I first set my eyes on sweet Moll - y Ma - lone, As she wheels her wheel barr - ow through streets broad and narr - ow, Cry - ing

She was a fishmonger, but sure 'twas no wonder,
For so were her father and mother before.
And they both wheeled their barrow.
Through streets broad and narrow,
Crying cockles and mussels, alive alive O!
CHORUS

She died of a fever and no one could save her,
And that was the end of sweet Molly Malone.
Now her ghost wheels her wheel barrow
Through streets broad and narrow,
Crying cockles and mussels, alive alive O!
CHORUS

She Lived Beside the Anner

Words by Charles J. Kickham

She lived be-side the An-ner at the foot of Slieve-na-mon, A gen-tle Ir-ish Col-leen with mild eyes like the dawn. Her lips were dew-y rose-buds, her teeth were pearls rare, And a

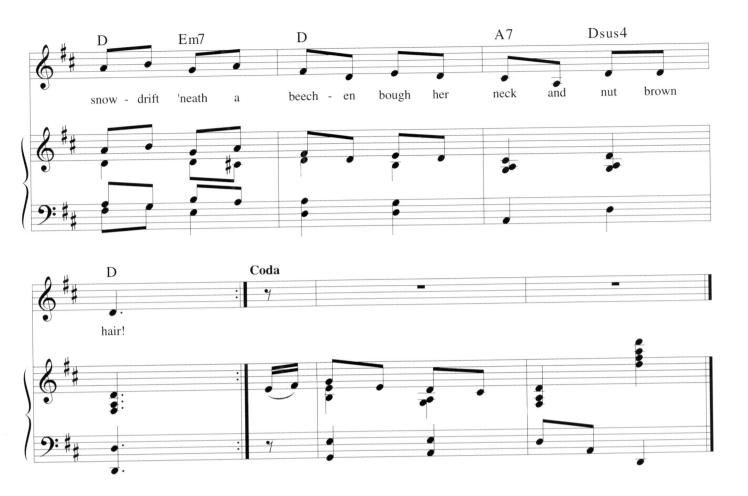

snow - drift 'neath a beech - en bough her neck and nut brown

hair!

Coda

How pleasant 'twas to see her on a Sunday when the bell
Was filling with its mellow tones lone wood and grassy dell!
And when at eve young maidens strayed the river bank along,
The widow's brown-haired daughter was the loveliest of the throng!

Oh! brave, brave Irish girls! We well may call you brave!
Sure the least of all your perils is the stormy ocean wave!
When you leave your quiet valleys and cross the Atlantic foam,
To save your hard-won earnings for the helpless ones at home!

Write word to my dear mother, say we'll meet with God above,
And tell my little brothers I send them all my love.
May angels ever guard them, is their dying sister's prayer!
And folded in the letter was a braid of nut-brown hair!

Ah! cold and well nigh callous this weary heart has grown,
For thy helpless fate, dear Ireland, and for sorrows of my own.
Yet a tear my eye will moisten, when by the Anner side I stray,
For the lily of the mountain foot that wither'd far away!

Slievenamon

Words by Charles J. Kickham

It was not the grace of her queenly air, nor her cheek of the rose's glow,
Nor her soft black eyes, nor her flowing hair, nor was it her lily-white brow.
'Twas the soul of truth and of melting ruth, and the smile like a summer dawn
That stole my heart away on a soft summer day in the Valley of Slievenamon.

In the festive hall by the sea-washed shore, my restless spirit cries,
My love, O my love shall I ne'er see you more? And my land, will you never uprise?
By night and by day I will ever, ever pray, as lonely this life goes on,
To see my flag unfurled and my true love to enfold, in the Valley of Slievenamon.

Love Thee Dearest

Words by Thomas Moore

Love thee, dear - est, love thee?

Yes! By yon - der star I swear, Which through tears a - bove thee

shines so sad - ly fair. Tho' too oft dim with tears like him, like

him my truth will shine, And love thee, dear - est, love thee?

Yes! Till death I'm thine.

No! Till death I'm thine.

Leave the, dearest, leave thee? No! That star is not more true,
When my vows deceive thee, he will wander too!
A cloud of night may veil his light, and death shall darken mine,
But leave thee dearest, leave thee? No! Till death I'm thine.

A Charabanc (Touring Coach) Gougane Barra, County Cork

The Rose of Aranmore

Traditional

My thoughts to - day, though I'm far a - way, dwell on Tyr - conn - ell's shore, The salt sea air and the

gown   of   green,   she's   the   rose   of   Ar - an -

more.   more.

I've travelled far 'neath the northern star since the day I said goodbye,
And seen many maids in the golden glades beneath a tropic sky.
There's a vision in my reverie I always will adore,
That grand colleen in her gown of green, she's the rose of Aranmore.

But soon I will return again to the scenes I loved so well,
Where an Irish lad and lass their tales of love do tell.
The silvery dunes and blue lagoons along the Rosses shore,
And that grand colleen in her gown of green, she's the rose of Aranmore.

Dan O'Hara

Adapted by Delia Murphy

Sure it's poor I am to-day for God gave and took a-
way, And He left with-out a home poor Dan O' Ha -
ra. With these match-es in my hand, in the frost and snow I

stand, So it's here I am to-day your brok-en-heart - ed.

Chorus A - chus-la geal mo chree, won't you buy a box from me, And you'll

have the prayers of Dan from Con - ne - ma - ra. I'll

sell them cheap and low, buy a box be - fore you go From the

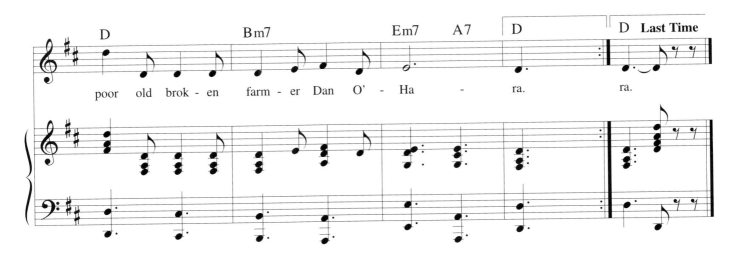

poor old brok - en farm - er Dan O' - Ha - ra. ra.

In the year of sixty-four I had acres by the score,
And the grandest land you ever ran a plough through.
But the landlord came you know, and he laid our old home low,
So it's here I am today your broken-hearted.
CHORUS

For twenty years or more did misfortune cross our door,
And my poor old wife and I were sadly parted.
We were scattered far and wide and our children starved and died,
So it's here I am today your broken-hearted.
CHORUS

Tho' in frost and snow I stand, sure the shadow of God's hand,
It lies warm about the brow of Dan O'Hara.
And soon with God above I will meet the ones I love,
And I'll find the joys I lost in Connemara.
CHORUS

Old Farm House, County Antrim

A Mother's Love Is a Blessing

Words & Music by Thomas P. Keenan

And as the years go onwards, I'll settle down in life,
And choose a nice young colleen and take her for my wife.
And as the babes grow older and climb around my knee,
I'll teach them the very same lesson as my mother taught to me:
CHORUS

The Old Rugged Cross

Words & Music by George Bernard

On a hill far a - way stands an old rug - ged Cross, The em - blem of suff - 'ring and pain, And I love that old Cross, where the no - blest and best, For a world of poor sin - ners was slain.

So I'll cher - ish that old rug - ged Cross, Till my

bur - den in life I lay down. I will

cling to that old rug - ged Cross, And I'll

change it one day for a crown.

To that old rugged Cross I will ever be true,
Its shame and reproach gladly bear,
Till He calls me some day to my home far away,
Where His Kingdom forever I'll share.
CHORUS

Now that old rugged Cross, so despised by the world,
Holds a strange, sweet attraction for me,
For the dear Lamb of God left His splendour above,
To bear it to dark Calvary.
CHORUS

In that old rugged Cross, stained with His precious blood,
A clear wondrous beauty I see,
For 'twas once on that Cross Jesus suffered and died,
To redeem and to sanctify me.
CHORUS

Celtic Cross

Bring Flowers of the Rarest (Queen of the May)

Traditional

tel - ling The praise of the love - li - est Flower of the Vale. O Ma - ry, we crown thee with blos - soms a - gain, Queen of the An - gels and Queen with - out stain. O Ma - ry we crown thee with blos - soms to -

Chorus

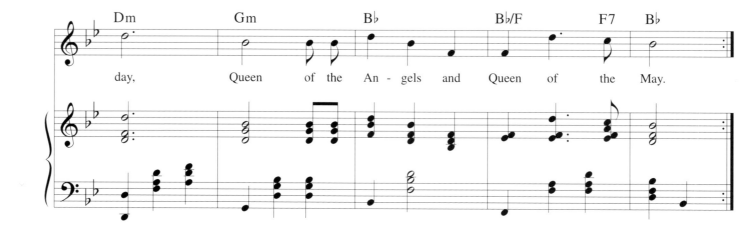

day, Queen of the An - gels and Queen of the May.

Their lady they name thee, their mistress proclaim thee,
Ah! grant that thy children on earth be as true.
As long as the bowers are radiant with flowers,
As long as the azure shall keep its bright hue.
CHORUS

Sing gaily in chorus, the bright angels o'er us
Re-echo the strain we begin upon earth.
Their harps are repeating the notes of our greeting,
For Mary herself is the cause of our mirth.
CHORUS

Our voices ascending, in harmony blending,
Oh, thus may our hearts turn, dear mother, to thee.
And thus shall we prove, dear, how truly we love thee,
How dark without Mary life's journey would be.
CHORUS

Noreen Bawn

Traditional

col - leen who in - spired the hearts of

men. She was hand - some, hale and

heart - y, shy and grace - ful like the

dawn, And they loved the wi - dow's

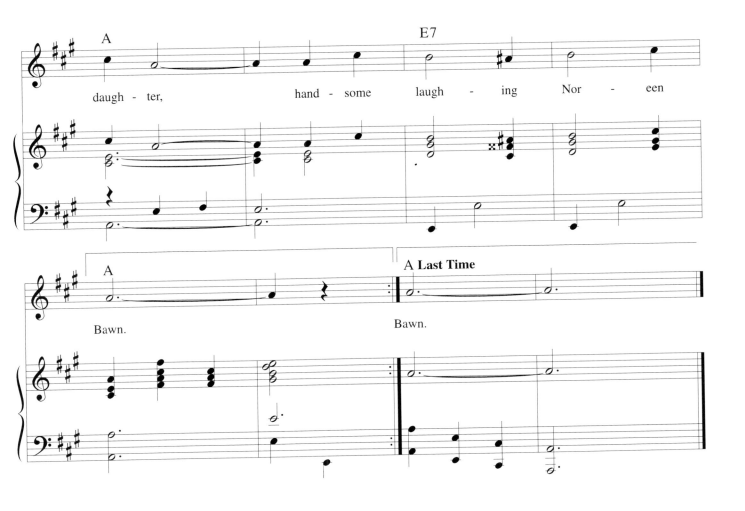

daugh - ter,   hand - some   laugh - ing   Nor - een

Bawn.   Bawn.

Till one day there came a letter with her passage paid to go,
To the land where the Missouri and the Mississippi flow.
So she said goodbye to Erin and next morning with the dawn,
This poor widow, broken-hearted, parted with her Noreen Bawn.

Many years the widow waited, till one morning to her door
Came a tender-hearted woman, costly were the clothes she wore,
Saying, 'Mother don't you know me, tho' I'm frail 'tis but a cold.
But her cheeks were flushed and scarlet and another tale they told.

There's a graveyard in Tir Connaill where the flowers wildly wave,
There's a grey-haired mother kneeling o'er a green and lonely grave.
'And my Noreen,' she is saying, 'it's been lonely since you've gone.
'Twas the curse of emigration laid you here my Noreen Bawn.'

Now fond youths and tender maidens, ponder well before you go
From humble homes in Erin, what's beyond you'll never know.
What is gold and what is silver when your health and strength are gone?
When they speak of emigration, won't you think of Noreen Bawn.

The Valley of Sweet Aherlow

Words & Music by Patrick J. Coughlan

When the moon's rid-ing high on Man - hat - tan

And there's gold on the Hud - son be - low, 'Mid the

glare and the lights of the ci - ty, I'm lone - ly, I'm

When I sit with my thoughts in the gloaming,
Dreaming dreams of the long, long ago,
Of the glens of my own Tipperary
In the shadow of old Galteemore,
I can see the blue mountains above me,
The corn waving mellow and gold,
The little green fields by the river,
In the valley of Sweet Aherlow.

I can count all the stiles and the bridges,
Down the road where the white thorn grows,
And the little thatched home by the roadside,
Where we sang 'round the fire long ago.
And I pray that the Lord hear my pining,
God grant that one day I'll go home
To the glens and the streams of my childhood,
In the valley of Sweet Aherlow.

Striking a Bargain

Bould Thady Quill

Traditional

Ye maids of Du - hal - low who're an - xious for court - ing, a word of ad - vice I will give un - to you. Pro - ceed to Ban - teer to the ath - let - ic sport - ing, and give in your names to the club com - mit - tee. And nev - er com - mence an - y

sketch of your prog - ramme till the carr - iage you see fly - ing ov - er the hill, Right

on thro' the val - leys and glens of Kil - corn - ey, with our dar - ling sports - man, our

Bould Thad - y Quill. For gambl - ing and bowl - ing, for foot - ball and court - ing, or

drain - ing a jor - um as fast as you'd fill, In all your days rov - ing you'd

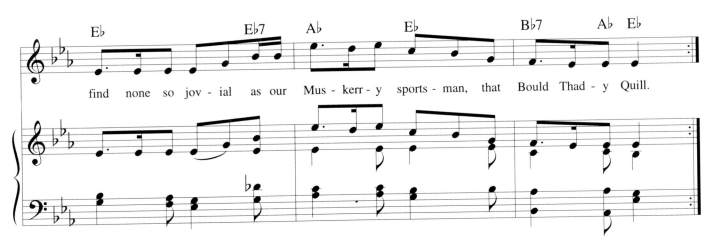

find none so jov-ial as our Mus-kerr-y sports-man, that Bould Thad-y Quill.

Let us sing of the fair golden vale of Tipperary, sing the praise and the fame of that Glen of Aherlow,
Where the goldfinch can thrill just like a canary, his song o'er the streams thro' the valley that flow.
They say that the Falls of Niagara thunder, that their sound with great fear all the listeners would fill,
But the Muskerry huntsmen would bate them no wonder, with one rousing whoop from Bould Thady Quill.
CHORUS

At the great hurling match between Cork and Tipperary, 'twas played in the park on the banks of the Lee.
Our own bravest boys were afraid of being beaten, so they sent for bould Thady to Ballinagree,
He hurled the ball right and to left in their faces, showed the boys from Tipp'rary both training and skill.
If they touched on his line he would certainly brain them, and they sang in the papers the praise of Thady Quill.
CHORUS

Some bucks once from Dublin came lookin' for trouble, with squireen from counties, adjacent likewise,
Swore they'd bate up Bould Thady, make him run 'at the double', and called all his exploits a parcel of lies.
But these foul allegations soon 'got up his dandher', and Bould Thady with great indignation did fill,
For he walloped them soundly, the price of the slander they hurled at ould Ireland and Bould Thady Quill.
CHORUS

Here's a health to the sportsmen of Ireland so merry, whose hearts are as stout and as brave as can be,
Who bate all the hurlers from Galway to Kerry, with their captain Bould Thady from Ballinagree.
For whether it's fightin' or courtin' or blarney, for teasin' and squeezin' our lad 'tops the bill'.
Sure all the fair colleens from here to Killarney are gone daft and crazy on Bould Thady Quill.
CHORUS

At the Cork Exhibition there was a fair lady, whose fortune exceeded a million or more,
But a poor constitution had ruined her completely, and 'Medical Treatment' had failed o'er and o'er.
'Ah, Mother,' said she, 'sure I know what will 'aise me, and cure the disease that will certainly kill.
Give over your doctors, your medical treatment, I'd sooner one squeeze out of Bould Thady Quill.'
CHORUS

In the year of ninety-one, before Parnell was taken, bould Thady was charged with a breach of the peace.
Though they put him in jail his heart was unshaken, with twelve months' hard labour for beating police.
But in spite of them all, Thady fought for our Nation, and the blood in his veins he's willing to spill,
To secure for old Ireland complete separation, and until that day comes there's no peace for Thady Quill.
CHORUS

The Moonshiner

Traditional

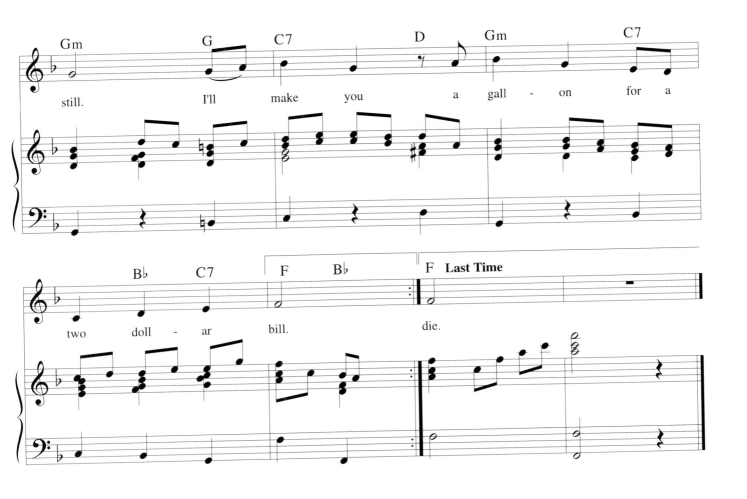

CHORUS:
I'm a rambler, I'm a gamber, I'm a long way from home,
If you don't like me, well leave me alone.
I'll eat when I'm hungry, I'll drink when I'm dry,
If moonshine won't kill me I'll live till I die.

I'll go to some hollow in this counterie,
Ten gallons of wash, I can go on the spree.
No woman to follow and the world is all mine,
I love none so well as I love the moonshine.
CHORUS

Moonshine, dear moonshine, oh how I love thee,
You kill'd my poor father but dare you try me,
Bless all moonshiners and bless all moonshine,
Its breath smells as sweet as the dew on the vine.
CHORUS

I'll have moonshine for Liza and moonshine for May,
Moonshine for Lu and she'll sing all the day,
Moonshine for my breakfast, moonshine for my tea,
Moonshine, my hearties, it's moonshine for me.
CHORUS

Connemara Lullaby

Words & Music by Liam Daly

There is a humble little home in Connemara,
And it is there my memories forever stray,
Back to those happy bygone days, and all the ones so loved.
In dreams I hear a mother gently say:
'When the sun had shed its glory and is sinking down to rest,
As night shades over Carna gently fall,
My thoughts keep turning to those loved ones who have sailed out West,
And their happy childhood days I still recall.
I pray that once again they'll gather 'round the open hearth,
But no, those dreams must surely fade and die.
Then mountain breezes lull a mother's tired and lonely heart to rest,
Like a haunting Connemara Lullaby.'

The Wild Colonial Boy

Adapted by Joseph Crofts

moth - er's pride and joy, And dear - ly did his par - ents love the

Wild Col - on - ial Boy. Boy. **Last Time**

At the hammer throwing Jack was great, or swinging a camán.
He led the boys in all their pranks, from dusk to early dawn.
At fishin' or at poachin' trout, he was the rale McCoy,
And all the neighbours loved young Jack, the Wild Colonial Boy.

At the early age of sixteen years he left his native home,
And to Australia's sunny land he was inclined to roam.
He robbed the rich and he helped the poor, he stabbed James MacEvoy.
A terror to Australia was the Wild Colonial Boy.

For two more years this daring youth ran on his wild career,
With a head that knew no danger, and a heart that knew no fear.
He robbed outright the wealthy squires, and their arms he did destroy,
And woe to all who dared to fight the Wild Colonial Boy.

He loved the Prairie and the Bush, where Rangers rode along,
With his gun stuck in its holster deep, he sang a merry song.
But if a foe once crossed his track, and sought him to destroy,
He'd get sharp shootin' sure from Jack, the Wild Colonial Boy.

One morning on the prairie, wild Jack Duggan rode along,
While listening to the mockingbird singing a cheerful song.
Out jumped three troopers, fierce and grim, Kelly, Davis and Fitzroy.
They all set out to capture him, the Wild Colonial Boy.

'Surrender now, Jack Duggan, Come! You see there's three to one!
Surrender to the Queen's name, Sir! You are a plundering Son!'
Jack drew a pistol from his side and drew upon Fitzroy.
'I'll fight, but not surrender!' cried the Wild Colonial Boy.

He fired a shot at Kelly, which brought him to the ground.
He fired point blank at Davis, too, who fell dead at the sound.
But a bullet pierced his brave young heart from the pistol of Fitzroy,
And that was how they captured him, the Wild Colonial Boy.